HANDS-ON HISTORY

PROJECTS ABOUT

Plantation Life

Marian Broida

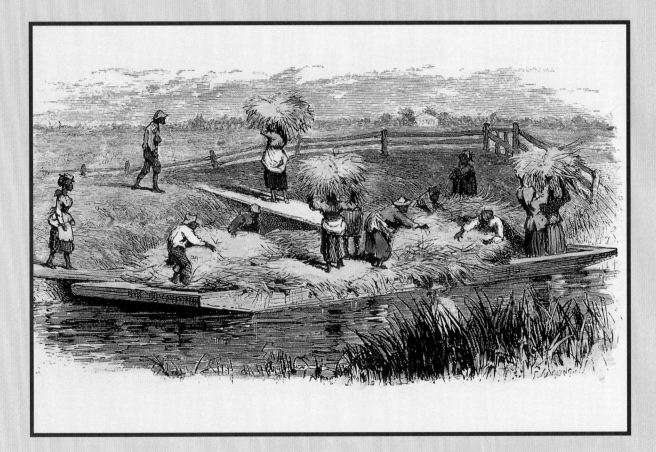

BENCHMARK BOOKS

MARSHALL CAVENDISH
NEW YORK

Acknowledgments

Tommy Brown, historian for Continental Eagle Corporation, Pratville, Alabama; Myra Castle, park manager, Florewood State Park, Mississippi; Martha B. Katz-Hyman, Colonial Williamsburg Foundation, Virginia; Marshall County Historical Museum, Holly Springs, Mississippi; Pat Veasey, director of education/interpretation, Historic Brattonsville, McConnells, South Carolina; Sivan Buchinsky, Beatrice Misher, and the View Ridge Boys' and Girls' Club for testing activities.

The cold remedy is adapted from the receipt book of Emily Sinkler, Charlestown, August 1, 1855. Published in *An Antebellum Plantation Household* by Anne Sinkler Whaley LeClercq, Columbia, SC: University of South Carolina Press, 1996, pp. 139–140.

The Graces Game is adapted from *Girls' Own Book* by Mrs. L. Maria Child, New York: Clark Austin & Co., 1833, pp. 105–106.

Benchmark Books
Marshall Cavendish
99 White Plains Road
Tarrytown, NY 10591-9001
www.marshallcavendish.com

Text copyright © 2004 by Marshall Cavendish Corporation
Illustrations © 2004 by Marshall Cavendish Corporation

Library of Congress Cataloging-in-Publication Data

Broida, Marian.
  Projects about plantation life / by Marian Broida.
    p. cm. — (Hands-on history)
Summary: Presents information about life in Virginia, South Carolina, and Mississippi between 1770 and 1860 and provides instructions for making such related projects as a Commonplace book, a folk remedy for colds, a recipe for Hoppin' John, and a girls' game called Graces.
Includes bibliographical references and index.
  ISBN 0-7614-1605-6
  1. Southern States—Social life and customs—1775-1865—Study and teaching—Activity programs—Juvenile literature. 2. Plantation life—Southern States—History—18th century—Study and teaching—Activity programs—Juvenile literature. 3. Plantation life—Southern States—History—19th century—Study and teaching—Activity programs—Juvenile literature. 4. Slaves—Southern States—Social life and customs—Study and teaching—Activity programs—Juvenile literature. 5. Plantation owners—Southern States—Social life and customs—Study and teaching—Activity programs—Juvenile literature. [1. Southern States—Social life and customs—1775-1865. 2. Plantation life—Southern States—History—19th century. 3. Handicraft.] I. Title. II. Series.

  F213.B757 2003
  975'.03—dc21

                          2003003822

Maps and Illustrations by Rodica Prato

Photo credits: *Corbis:* 4. *Bettmann/Corbis:* 10. *Hulton-Deutsch collection/Corbis:* 28. *Hulton Archive by Getty Images:* 34. *North Wind Picture Archives:* 1, 12, 22, 32.

Printed in China

1 3 5 6 4 2

Contents

◆

After the Civil War this group of freed slaves gathered on a South Carolina plantation that had been owned by a Confederate general. The former slaves stayed on and ran the cotton business for their own profit.

1

Introduction

❦

Do you see green fields of young tobacco?

Feel the burning hot sun of summer? Smell sweet potatoes baking in the ashes of a fireplace?

In this book you will travel back in time to experience life on plantations, large farms in southern America where workers raised crops for sale. From the 1600s until the **Civil War**, **plantations** were an important part of Southern life, producing tobacco, rice, sugar, cotton, and other crops.

Very few Southerners owned plantations, but many lived on them. Plantation owners, called **planters**, were among the wealthiest people in the South. Most workers were enslaved African men, women, and children. The slaves owned no property and were themselves thought to be the property of their masters. You will learn about daily life among slave and planter families. You will visit a tobacco plantation in the colony of Virginia around the year 1770, a rice plantation in South Carolina about 1850, and a cotton plantation in Mississippi around 1860, just before the Civil War.

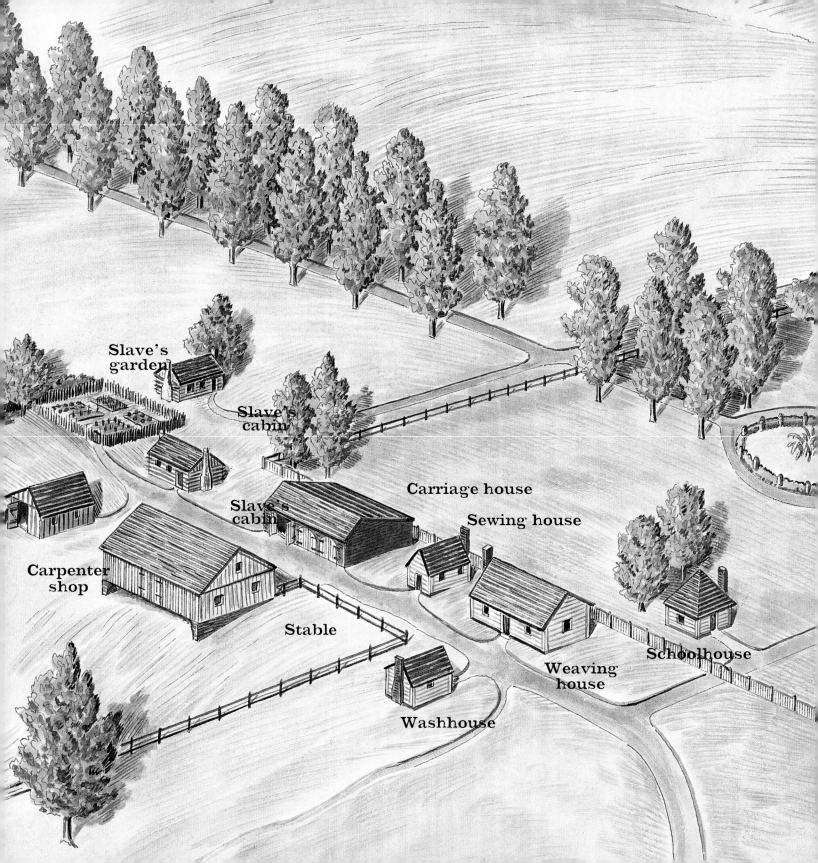

Slave's garden

Slave's cabin

Slave's cabin

Carpenter shop

Carriage house

Sewing house

Stable

Washhouse

Weaving house

Schoolhouse

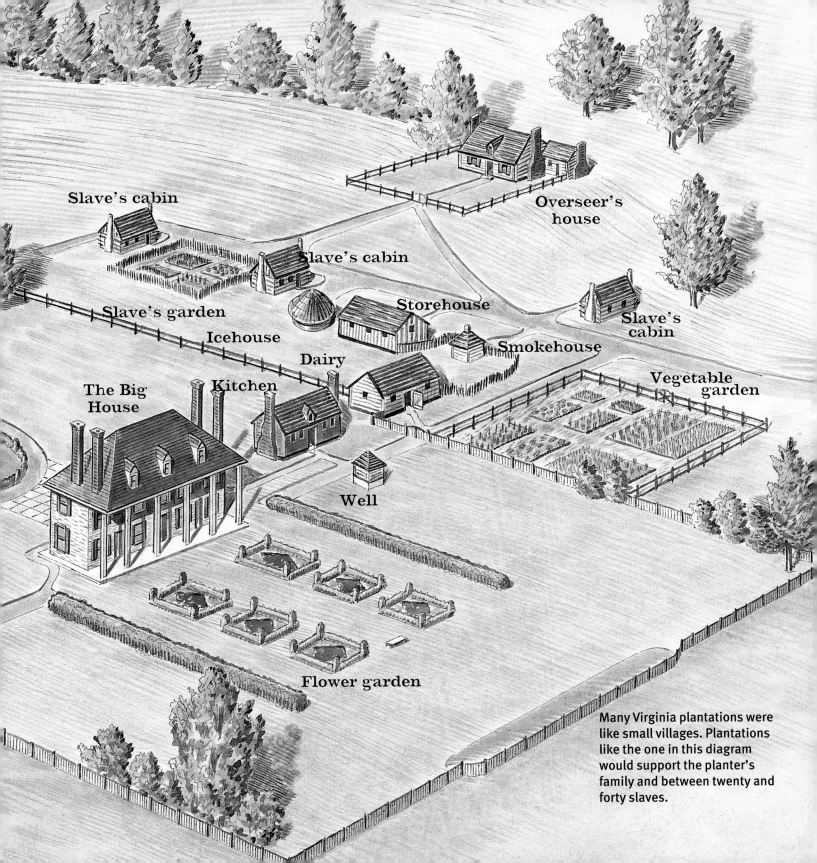

Slave's cabin

Slave's cabin

Overseer's house

Slave's garden

Slave's cabin

Icehouse

Storehouse

Smokehouse

Dairy

Vegetable garden

Kitchen

The Big House

Well

Flower garden

Many Virginia plantations were like small villages. Plantations like the one in this diagram would support the planter's family and between twenty and forty slaves.

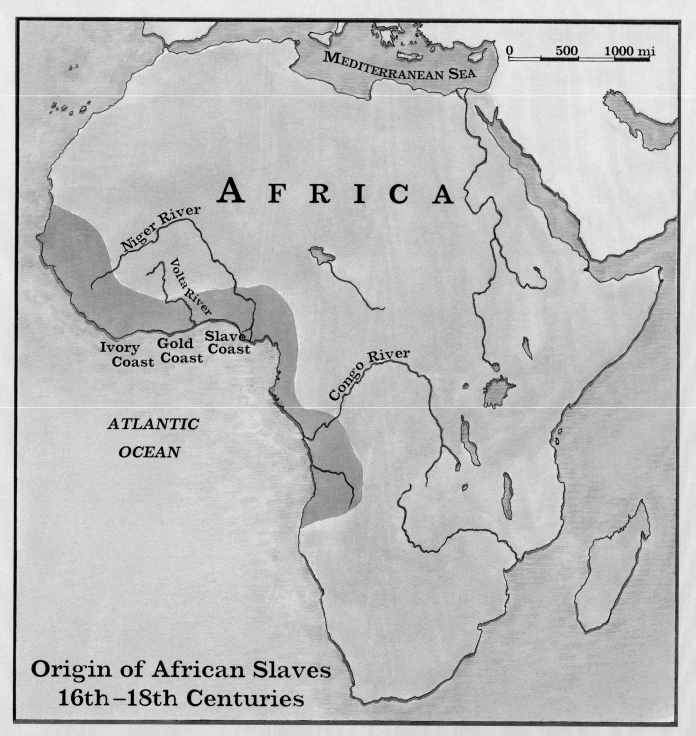

0　500　1000 mi

MEDITERRANEAN SEA

AFRICA

Niger River

Volta River

Ivory Coast

Gold Coast

Slave Coast

Congo River

ATLANTIC

OCEAN

Origin of African Slaves
16th–18th Centuries

Most slaves came from West Africa—specifically, the regions shown as the shaded area on this map—the part of Africa closest to the Americas. Slave ships sometimes carried as many as six hundred people at a time. As many as 10 to 15 percent would die before reaching North America.

CANADA

Minnesota

Nebraska

Territory

Wisconsin

Maine

VT

NH

MA

CT

RI

Iowa

Michigan

New York

Kansas

Territory

Illinois

Ohio

Pennsylvania

New Jersey

Delaware

Indiana

West
Virginia

Mexico

itory

Indian

Territory

Missouri

Kentucky

Virginia

Arkansas

Tennessee

North
Carolina

Texas

Mississippi

Alabama

South
Carolina

Georgia

ATLANTIC

Louisiana

OCEAN

Florida

GULF OF MEXICO

Free state or territory
Slave state or territory

This map shows the states and **territories** that allowed slavery in 1860, the year before the Civil War began.
Most North American plantations were located in these slave-tolerant states.

When George Washington inherited Mount Vernon, the estate covered approximately 2,000 acres. At the time of his death in 1799, it had grown to almost 8,000 acres.

2
Virginia, 1770

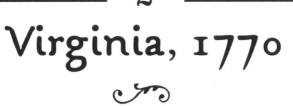

Virginia was home to some of the colonies' first plantations. Early Virginia plantations were often small, with **indentured servants** working the fields. By 1770 plantations were much larger, growing tobacco, wheat, and corn. At that time enslaved Africans provided almost all the labor, while the planters took the profits.

Most workers did farmwork and were called field slaves. Others, called house slaves, took care of the planter's home and family. Most slaves lived in buildings called **quarters**. The planter's family lived in a **mansion** called the Great House or Big House.

Planters gave slaves cheap food and clothing, but no money for their regular work. Many plantation owners let slaves raise their own vegetables and chickens to eat or to sell. Some Virginia slaves spent the money they earned on jewelry or clothing. Others saved it to buy their freedom, when it was allowed.

Many famous founders of the United States owned plantations, including George Washington and Thomas Jefferson. These men had much to say about liberty when they talked about freedom from England. But few thought that slaves should have the same freedom as their owners.

George Washington was a kinder master than most. Unlike many planters, he was reluctant to punish his slaves by having them beaten. He also refused to sell his slaves, since that would break up their families. Washington's will provided for his slaves to be freed after his death. But he did not oppose slavery enough to free them while he lived.

Slave Quarters

You are watching your father, a carpenter, build a log cabin with two other slaves. They are covering the wooden chimney with clay to keep it from catching fire.

Slave cabins in Virginia around 1770 were often built of logs. These one-room dwellings with dirt floors were shared by as many as twelve people.

Your family will live in the cabin when it is done. Right now you are sharing a cabin with another family—ten people in one room. It is hard to find a place on the floor to sleep.

The **overseer** comes by to supervise. He says nothing, but you can tell he approves of the men's work.

You will need:

- newspaper
- pot you do not need for food
- 1 cup cornstarch
- 2 cups play sand (available from hardware store)
- large spoon you do not need for food
- 1½ cups warm water
- stove
- pot holders
- sturdy dinner-size paper plate, 8 or more inches across on the flat part of the base
- paper towel
- corrugated cardboard, 21 by 4 inches
- yardstick or meterstick
- pencil
- scissors
- empty half-gallon milk or orange juice carton, clean and dry
- duct tape
- brown tempera or acrylic paint
- paintbrushes
- corrugated cardboard, about 7 by 2 inches
- corrugated cardboard, about 2 inches square

1. Ask an adult to help you make fake dirt.

2. Lay the newspaper down on your work surface.

3. Mix the cornstarch and sand in the pot with the large spoon. Stir in the water. Cook on medium heat, stirring frequently, until the mixture gets thick, about 8 minutes.

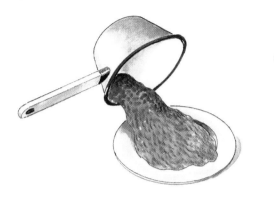

4. Using the pot holders, empty the sand mixture onto the plate over the newspaper. Cover the mixture with a damp paper towel, and let cool.

5. Meanwhile, lay the biggest piece of cardboard along the yardstick the long way, so it reaches from the end of the ruler to the 21-inch mark. (If there is writing on the cardboard, place that side faceup.) Mark the cardboard at 2 inches, 7 inches, 14 inches, and 19 inches.

6. Using the yardstick, draw a straight line across the cardboard at every mark you made. Press hard with the pencil.

7. Fold the cardboard at each line. Important: all the folds go the same way, toward the inside (see illustration). When you stand the folded cardboard on its edge, it should look like a square C-shape from above.

8. Throw away the paper towel. Smooth the fake dirt. Place the folded cardboard on top of the dirt, and press it in firmly. Build up the dirt around the walls, inside and out, to hold them firmly in place. You now have a little room with a doorway.

9. Dig down to the plate to make a **root cellar**.

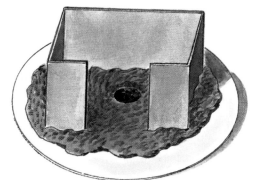

10. Cut the top off the milk carton and throw it away. Now cut a slit along one edge from one corner to the base. Do the same along the OPPOSITE edge (not the edge next to the one you just cut).

11. Cut across the base in a straight line between the two corners you just slit. You should now have two triangle-shaped halves.

12. Choose one half for the roof. Cut the triangular base off the OTHER half. Tape the triangle onto the open end of the roof, using duct tape on the inside. (Have someone help hold the roof steady.)

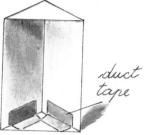

duct tape

13. Paint the roof brown. Paint brown stripes on the cabin walls, from side to side, to look like logs.

14. When the paint is dry, set the roof on top of the walls. Stand the 7-by-2-inch strip of cardboard next to one end, for a chimney. Tape the chimney to the end of the roof (not to the building) with duct tape. Paint the duct tape and the chimney brown.

duct tape

15. Cover the root cellar with the small cardboard square.

16. To look inside the house, lift off the roof.

Commonplace Book

In the parlor of the Great House, your father hands you a small, blank book.

"I am giving you this so that you may start a **commonplace book**," he says. "In it you must write down things you read or hear that you find valuable. Lines from poems or sermons, or advice from your elders. Writing them will help fix them in your memory."

"Thank you, Father," you say.

Your father shows you another book. "This is a commonplace book I kept in my youth." He smiles. "Not everything you write must be serious. See, here is a riddle I wrote: "Why do we all go to bed?""

"Because the bed will not come to us!" you answer.

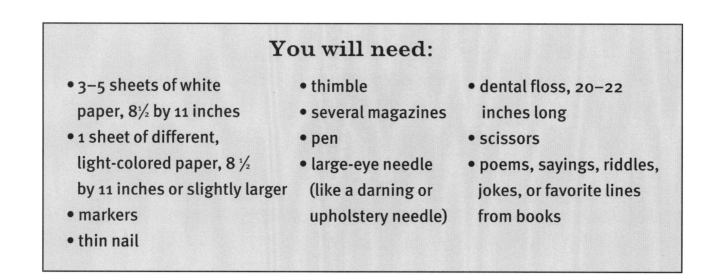

You will need:

- 3–5 sheets of white paper, 8½ by 11 inches
- 1 sheet of different, light-colored paper, 8 ½ by 11 inches or slightly larger
- markers
- thin nail

- thimble
- several magazines
- pen
- large-eye needle (like a darning or upholstery needle)

- dental floss, 20–22 inches long
- scissors
- poems, sayings, riddles, jokes, or favorite lines from books

1. Separately fold each sheet of white paper in half widthwise, making a rectangle 5½ by 8½ inches. Press firmly to make sharp creases. Open the pages, and stack them as shown.

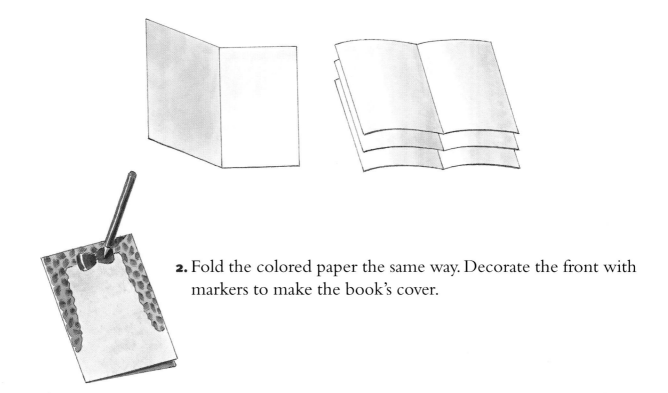

2. Fold the colored paper the same way. Decorate the front with markers to make the book's cover.

3. Open the cover and lay the pages on top so all the creases stack up and all the pages open toward you.

4. Stack the magazines, and place your open book on top. The magazines will protect the table. With the pen, mark four dots, evenly spaced, along the inner crease. (The first and last dots should be at least 1 inch from each edge.)

5. Wearing the thimble on your thumb, poke the nail through each dot.

6. Thread the needle with the floss. You may have to ask an adult for help.

7. Poke the needle through the lowest hole, front to back. Pull most of the floss through, leaving a tail at least 4 inches long.

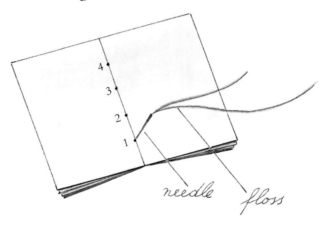

needle   *floss*

8. Poke the needle through the next hole up, back to front. Pull the floss through without shortening the tail. Make sure the tail stays long as you continue.

9. Poke the needle through the third hole up, front to back. Pull the floss through.

10. Poke through the top hole from back to front.

11. Now poke the needle through the third hole again, front to back.

12. Stick the needle through the second hole up, from back to front. Unthread the needle.

13. Tie the two tails of floss together with a double knot or square knot. Trim the ends.

14. Copy parts of your favorite books, poems, sayings, and jokes into your commonplace book. Use your best handwriting.

Yoke for Carrying Water

The overseer tells you to carry water to the slaves working in the south field. "Use the yoke," he says.

You fill two wooden buckets at the well and fasten one to each end of the wooden yoke. Now you crouch and slide the yoke over your shoulders, behind your neck. You stand slowly, feeling the strain in your shoulders, neck, and back.

"Now go on," he says. "Don't let me see you lagging!"

It is hard to stand upright, and even harder to walk. You move slowly to keep the water from spilling. The overseer frowns. "Lazy!" he says, raising his hand. You cringe.

You will need:

- 2 clean, empty margarine tubs, 16-ounce size, without lids
- pen
- 2 pipe cleaners
- a one-hole punch
- two 18-inch pieces of yarn
- 3-foot dowel or yardstick
- Scotch tape
- two cans of tuna fish
- jar with several cups of water

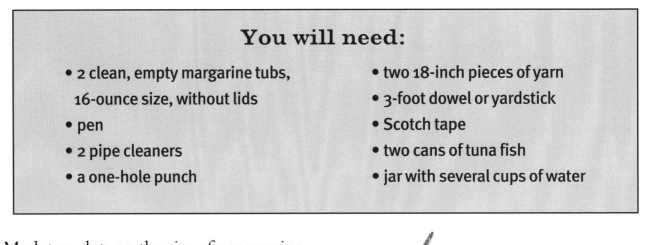

1. Mark two dots on the rim of a margarine tub, straight across from each other. You can do this by laying a pipe cleaner on top of the tub, right in the middle. Hold it in place (or have a friend hold it), and make a dot on the rim under each end. Remove the pipe cleaner.

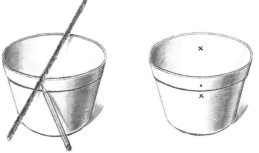

2. Punch a hole in the rim on each side, below each dot, at least ½ inch from the top.

3. Thread one end of a piece of yarn through a hole, and tie it in place with a double knot or square knot, as shown. Fasten the other end of the yarn in the other hole.

4. Repeat steps 1 through 3 with the other tub.

5. Dangle one "bucket" by its yarn handle. Loop it over the dowel, about 2 inches from the end. Make sure it hangs straight.

6. Tape it in place.

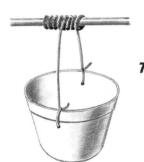

7. Wrap a pipe cleaner around the dowel, over the tape, to hold the tape in place. Start with the end of the pipe cleaner. Hold the pipe cleaner still with one hand while you wrap with the other.

8. Repeat steps 5 through 7 with the other "bucket," at the other end of the dowel.

9. Place the yoke behind your neck, one bucket hanging on each side. Hold on to the dowel with your hands.

10. Practice by carrying a can of tuna in each bucket. Then remove the cans and have a friend fill each bucket halfway with water as you hold the yoke. How far can you carry it without spilling?

The many steps involved in planting, growing, harvesting, and preparing rice for market required a very large number of slaves. Each individual usually worked at backbreaking tasks for nine to ten hours a day.

3

South Carolina, 1850

Rice plantations flourished on the coast of South Carolina. By the 1800s many South Carolina plantations also grew cotton.

Life on plantations meant work for everyone, not just the slaves. The planter, who was usually a man, bought or sold crops and equipment. The plantation mistress, usually the planter's wife, took care of the household. She made sure that there was enough food and clothing, the laundry was done, and the house was kept clean. The planter's children studied with tutors or in private schools. Girls and boys were educated differently, although both learned to read and write. Girls were taught skills such as singing and sewing to help them attract husbands and learn to manage a household. Boys were expected to learn more school subjects such as geography and science.

South Carolina slaves kept African traditions longer than Virginia slaves did. Among themselves, slaves in South Carolina told folktales, sang songs, and cooked favorite foods from their homelands, such as **black-eyed peas** and **okra**. Enslaved cooks sometimes used these foods when cooking for the planters' families. Those foods became an important part of southern cooking.

Cooking Hoppin' John

It is New Year's Day. Mistress has sent you to the kitchen to help the cook make dinner for the planter's family. The cook, another slave, is boiling black-eyed peas with salt pork and rice.

"This is Hoppin' John, like my granny used to make in the quarters," the cook tells you. "She said, 'If you eat Hoppin' John on New Year's Day, you have good luck all year.'"

"I know what good luck would be," you say. "Running away North, and getting there safe."

"Hush," says the cook. "Don't you know better than to say that right out, where anyone could hear you?"

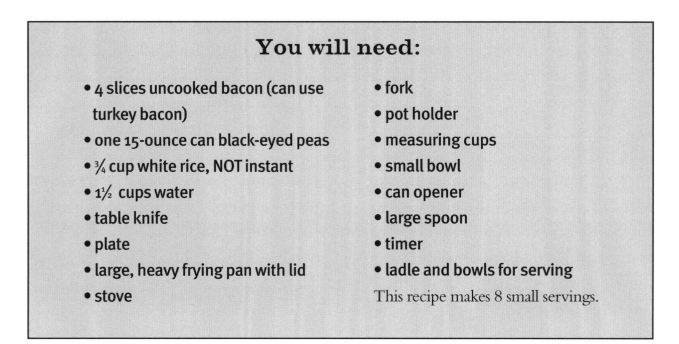

You will need:

- 4 slices uncooked bacon (can use turkey bacon)
- one 15-ounce can black-eyed peas
- ¾ cup white rice, NOT instant
- 1½ cups water
- table knife
- plate
- large, heavy frying pan with lid
- stove
- fork
- pot holder
- measuring cups
- small bowl
- can opener
- large spoon
- timer
- ladle and bowls for serving

This recipe makes 8 small servings.

1. Have an adult help you. Wash your hands.

2. Cut the bacon strips in half on the plate, and put them in the frying pan.

3. Fry the bacon strips on low heat. When they curl, turn them over with the fork. Use the pot holder to hold the pan handle.

4. Measure the rice and the water into the measuring cups.

5. Open the can of black-eyed peas with the can opener. When the bacon edges begin to brown, carefully empty the black-eyed peas into the pan. (Stand back so the fat doesn't splatter you.)

6. Cook on low heat, stirring occasionally with the large spoon, for two minutes.

7. Add the rice and stir. Add the water, and mix well.

8. Turn the heat to high, until the mixture boils. Then cover the pan and turn the heat to low. Set the timer for fifteen minutes.

9. When the timer sounds, look inside the pot, but don't stir. Fork up a rice grain to nibble. (Be careful. It will be hot.) If the rice is too crunchy, turn off the stove and let the pot sit, covered, another five minutes. If it is not crunchy, remove the rice from the heat. When the rice is done, you can serve right away.

10. To serve, ladle out the peas and rice into bowls. Place a piece of bacon on top of each serving.

Cold Remedy

"I think you may be coming down with a cold," says your Mother. "I'll give you a dose of mercury and chalk." As the plantation mistress, she is in charge of the family's health, and the slaves' as well.

"Please, Mother, no!" you beg. "I don't want any nasty-tasting medicine!"

"All right," says your mother. "I've heard of another way to cut short a cold, without medicine. But you must be patient and do it properly. I'll send Sukey up to help."

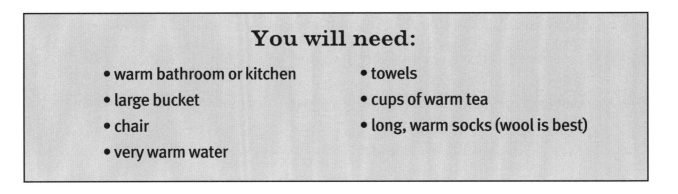

You will need:

- warm bathroom or kitchen
- large bucket
- chair
- very warm water
- towels
- cups of warm tea
- long, warm socks (wool is best)

Try this remedy at the first sign of a cold. Talk to your parents before trying any home treatments.

1. Ask an adult for help.

2. In a warm bathroom or kitchen, fill a bucket halfway with very warm water. Test it to make sure it is not painfully hot.

3. Take off your shoes and socks, and roll up your pants.

4. Sit in the chair with your legs in the bucket. The water should be halfway to your knees. Have towels handy. Stay there for fifteen minutes. Empty and refill the bucket whenever the water cools.

5. While your feet soak, have your helper bring you a cup or two of warm tea.

6. After fifteen minutes remove your feet and dry them thoroughly. Put on warm socks, even in the summer.

7. Drink lots of liquids, and stay warm for the next twenty-four hours. If the remedy works, your cold should go away quickly.

Boys' Play: Marbles and Ringtaw Game

You and your brother are walking to the plantation schoolhouse. Near the stable you pass two slave boys playing with clay marbles.

"Let me see that shooter," your brother says, plunking down beside them.

"Come on, Tom, we'll be late!" you say.

Tom ignores you and picks up the biggest marble. "This looks just like the shooter I lost last week. Did one of you steal it?"

"No, Master Tom, I made it from river clay," says one of the boys, looking terrified. "But you keep it, sir, if you want it."

Tom shoves the marble in his pocket and stands up. "We'd better hurry," he tells you.

The game of marbles has been played for many years by children around the world. These boys are playing in a backyard in England around 1860.

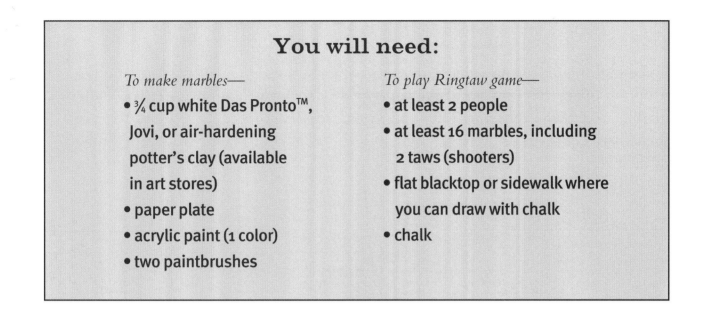

You will need:

To make marbles—
- ¾ cup white Das Pronto™, Jovi, or air-hardening potter's clay (available in art stores)
- paper plate
- acrylic paint (1 color)
- two paintbrushes

To play Ringtaw game—
- at least 2 people
- at least 16 marbles, including 2 taws (shooters)
- flat blacktop or sidewalk where you can draw with chalk
- chalk

1. First, make the marbles.

2. Place the clay on the paper plate. If using potter's clay, throw it down on the plate and knead it a few times to get out any air bubbles.

3. Pull off a small piece. Roll it between your palms to shape a ball the size of a regular marble. Make at least sixteen balls this size. Make another two about as wide across as quarters, to be taws, or shooters.

4. Leave the marbles on the plate until they dry. This may take up to one week.

5. Once they are dry, paint eight marbles and one taw a different color. Pour about 1 teaspoon of acrylic paint on a large paper plate. Using two paintbrushes, roll the marbles and taw in the paint. Then roll them over dry areas of the plate to wipe off the excess. Let them dry, turning them at least once while drying or they will stick to the plate.

6. Then play the game. Ask at least one friend to join you. Get permission to draw on the ground, then draw a circle about 1 foot across.

7. Draw a straight line 2 to 3 feet away from the circle, as shown.

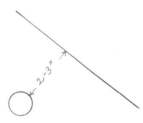

8. To play, each person puts five or more normal-size marbles in the circle.

9. Decide who shoots first. Then decide if you are playing "for keeps." If you are, you get to keep the marbles you hit. Otherwise you have to return them to their owners after the game. This is easier if each person's marbles look different.

10. To start, place your "shooting" hand on the ground just behind the line. To shoot, lay the taw on your forefinger, in the crook between your fingertip and your middle knuckle. (See illustration.) Flick the taw with the back of your thumb so it rolls toward the circle. Do not move the rest of your hand.

11. Your goal is to hit marbles out of the ring and have your taw stop out of the ring. Then you get to keep the marbles that you hit out of the ring. Shoot again from wherever your taw landed.

12. If your taw does not enter the ring, your turn is over. Next time shoot from wherever your taw stopped.

13. If your taw stays in the ring, whether or not you hit another marble, your turn is over. Leave your taw there. You get to keep any marbles you hit out of the ring. Next time shoot from behind the line again, using another marble.

14. If another player's taw hits your taw, inside or outside of the ring, you must give the other player any marbles you have won so far during that game. The other player's turn continues.

15. The game ends when all the marbles have been hit out of the ring. The player who has the most marbles wins.

16. If you get really good, next time draw the line farther from the circle.

BALING COTTON.

This illustration shows the various stages of processing cotton with steam power.

4

Mississippi, 1860

The few plantations that existed in Mississippi before the 1790s grew only tobacco. But the invention of the **cotton gin** made it worthwhile for planters to raise cotton. The cotton gin was a machine that removed seeds from cotton. This meant that planters could produce more cotton with less manpower. Everywhere in the South, planters began growing "white gold."

In the 1830s the United States government forced Mississippi's Choctaw and Chickasaw Indians to give up their lands and move west. More planters rushed into Mississippi with their slaves to start large cotton plantations.

Many Mississippi planters grew wealthy. They lived in mansions, held elegant parties, and followed strict rules of hospitality and manners. Their comfortable lives lasted until the Civil War. During and after the war, planters lost much of what they owned. But their slaves gained something far more precious: their freedom.

Calling Cards

You climb out of your carriage in front of an elegant mansion. "Wait here," you tell the driver.

You go up the steps, then cross the **veranda** to the door. A familiar servant welcomes you into a grand entryway.

"James," you say, "I've come to call on Miss Greenway."

The servant bows his head and says he is sorry but Miss Greenway is out.

"Then I'll leave her my card," you say, opening your tiny silver card case. You place a card printed with your name in a dish on a small table. "Ah," you say, peering at another card in the dish. "I see that Mr. Cole has already called."

A slave announces the arrival of a visitor to the master of the house. Paying visits and receiving guests were at the center of plantation social life. All guests were welcomed and treated to the best food and lodging the host had to offer.

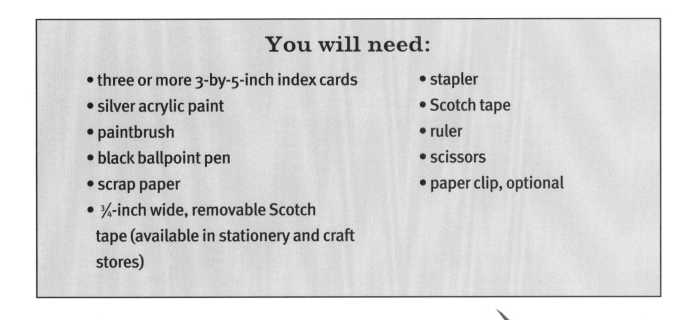

You will need:

- three or more 3-by-5-inch index cards
- silver acrylic paint
- paintbrush
- black ballpoint pen
- scrap paper
- ¾-inch wide, removable Scotch tape (available in stationery and craft stores)

- stapler
- Scotch tape
- ruler
- scissors
- paper clip, optional

1. First, make a case for your cards. Paint the unlined side of an index card silver. While it dries, practice writing your full name in fancy script on scrap paper.

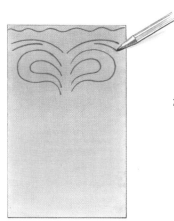

2. When the card is dry, draw curlicues, flowers, and other decorations in pen on the silver side.

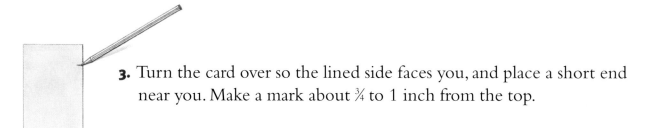

3. Turn the card over so the lined side faces you, and place a short end near you. Make a mark about ¾ to 1 inch from the top.

4. Gently fold the bottom end up to where it meets the mark. Don't press hard on the fold.

5. Fold the upper end over, as shown, making a little packet, silver side out.

6. Draw a little line where the edge of the top flap hits the bottom flap. Open the top flap.

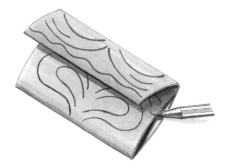

7. Tear off a piece of removable tape, 2 to 3 inches long. Cut it in half lengthwise.

8. Lay one half, sticky side up, just above the line. Discard the other half.

9. Staple the tape in place with 4 to 5 staples in a row. (Have someone hold the case steady.)

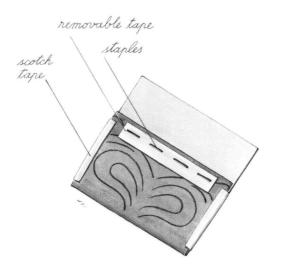

10. Tape the left and right sides of the bottom flap closed with regular Scotch tape, from top to bottom as shown. Trim any excess tape.

11. Now make calling cards. Cut the other two index cards into rectangles that fit easily inside your case (about 2½ by 1½ inches). Write your name elegantly on each card, with lots of curly lines. Ladies' cards often had drawings of flowers.

12. If the removable tape wears out, slit one side of the case (so the stapler can fit in) and replace it, or use a paper clip to hold the case shut.

Miniature Cotton Bale

Your uncle, a slave, is telling you about how he runs the plantation **cotton press**.

"What that machine does," he says, "is take loose cotton and squeeze it into bundles called bales."

"Tell me what you do," you say.

"First, we lay out **burlap** cloth inside a box and dump in some cotton," he says. "Then, a man drives a team of mules in a circle. Those mules are hitched to a great big screw hanging over the box. When the mules move, that screw comes down and squashes the cotton flat. We keep adding cotton and bringing down the screw until the box is packed. Then we take out the cotton, burlap and all, and fasten it around with metal bands. That's a bale. It weighs more than you and the other children together."

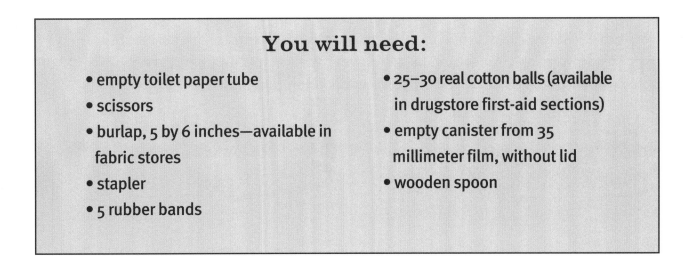

You will need:

- empty toilet paper tube
- scissors
- burlap, 5 by 6 inches—available in fabric stores
- stapler
- 5 rubber bands
- 25–30 real cotton balls (available in drugstore first-aid sections)
- empty canister from 35 millimeter film, without lid
- wooden spoon

1. First, make your cotton press. Cut 1 to 1½ inches off the end of a toilet paper tube. Keep the larger part.

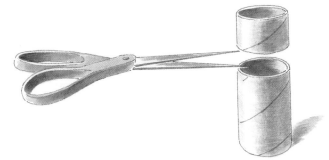

2. Pull the burlap through the tube the long way, so the 6-inch sides lie along the walls of the tube. Smooth out the burlap so it forms a tube inside the cardboard tube, with cloth sticking out at each end.

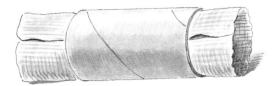

3. Staple the burlap tube closed at one end. Do not staple the sides, even if they do not quite meet.

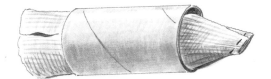

4. Push the toilet paper tube down so the bottom is at the stapled end. Stand the tube on that end, on a firm surface.

5. Now prepare your cotton. Pull apart the cotton balls with your fingers, until you have a single pile of cotton lint. Pretend it has just come from the cotton gin, where the seeds were removed.

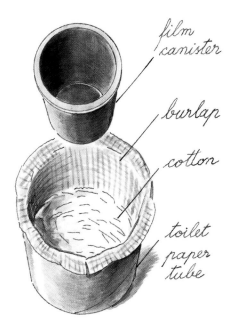

film canister

burlap

cotton

toilet paper tube

6. Stuff some lint into the open burlap tube. Place the film canister on top, open side up. Put your fingers or the handle of the wooden spoon inside the canister, and mash the cotton down inside the toilet paper tube.

7. Repeat step 6 until you've used all the cotton. Remove the film canister.

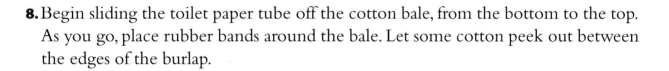

8. Begin sliding the toilet paper tube off the cotton bale, from the bottom to the top. As you go, place rubber bands around the bale. Let some cotton peek out between the edges of the burlap.

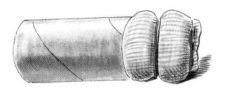

9. Fold down the top end of the burlap, as shown, and fasten with another rubber band.

Girls' Play: The Graces Game

Your sisters are laughing and tossing a ribbon-wrapped hoop back and forth, using two pairs of sticks.

"What are you playing?" you ask.

"It's called the Graces," says your older sister. "Mother thinks it provides the proper sort of exercise for young ladies."

"It looks easy," you say. "Give me your sticks."

You hold them upright while your other sister tosses you the hoop. It bounces off your sticks and clatters to the floor.

"This is not the proper sort of exercise for me," you say.

You will need:

- newspaper
- 4 pieces of dowel, each 18 inches long
- sandpaper, optional
- embroidery hoop (inner hoop only), about 8 inches across (available in fabric and craft stores)
- 5–6 feet of ribbon, ¼ inch wide
- 5–6 feet of ribbon in another color, any width, cut in half to make 2 shorter pieces
- Scotch tape
- scissors

1. Spread the newspaper on your work surface, then sand any rough spots on the dowels.

2. Tape the end of the 5-foot ribbon to the hoop. Wrap the ribbon snugly around and around the hoop, leaving a little space between wrappings.

3. When you have finished wrapping, tuck the end under one of the earlier loops. Trim it. Tape it down securely.

4. Tie the two shorter pieces of ribbon to the hoop, right next to each other. Let the ends hang down as streamers.

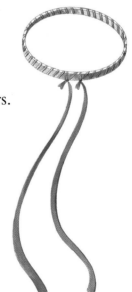

To Play the Graces Game

1. Ask at least one friend to play.

2. Each player takes two sticks. Stand several feet apart.

3. To throw the hoop, cross the sticks and lay the hoop over them, as shown. Use the sticks to toss the hoop.

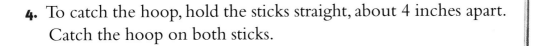

4. To catch the hoop, hold the sticks straight, about 4 inches apart. Catch the hoop on both sticks.

5. To make the game more difficult, move farther apart.

Glossary

black-eyed peas: Edible beans with a black spot.

burlap: The coarse brown cloth used to make sacks and wrap cotton bales.

Civil War: Conflict from 1861 to 1865 between the Northern states (the Union) and Southern states (the Confederacy) that began when the Southern states decided to form their own country. The main issue was slavery. Also called the War Between the States.

commonplace book: A kind of journal in which people wrote down notes and favorite lines from their reading.

cotton bales: Bundles of tightly pressed cotton. In the past, bales were usually wrapped in burlap and fastened with rope or metal bands. Bales weigh hundreds of pounds.

cotton gin: The machine that removes seeds from cotton.

cotton press: The machine that squeezes cotton into bales.

indentured servants: In colonial times, persons bound to work for someone for a number of years. In exchange, their trip from Europe to the colonies was paid for.

mansion: An elegant house.

okra: A plant from West Africa with edible green pods used in soups and stews.

overseer: A white man hired to make sure slaves worked hard and did not escape.

plantations: A large farm where workers (servants or slaves) grew crops for the owner to sell.

planters: Owners of plantations, usually white men, sometimes called the master, or the mistress, if a woman.

root cellar: A square hole in the ground used to store root vegetables. Inside some slave cabins, slaves used root cellars to keep food, small tools, jewelry, and other treasured possessions.

quarters: Slaves' houses on a plantation.

territories: Areas that had not yet become states.

veranda: A wide porch with a roof.

Metric Conversion Chart

You can use the chart below to convert from U. S. measurements to the metric system.

Weight
1 ounce = 28 grams
½ pound (8 ounces) = 227 grams
1 pound = .45 kilogram
2.2 pounds = 1 kilogram

Liquid volume
1 teaspoon = 5 milliliters
1 tablespoon = 15 milliliters
1 fluid ounce = 30 milliliters
1 cup = 240 milliliters (.24 liter)
1 pint = 480 milliliters (.48 liter)
1 quart = .95 liter

Length
¼ inch = .6 centimeter
½ inch = 1.25 centimeters
1 inch = 2.5 centimeters

Temperature
100°F = 40°C
110°F = 45°C
350°F = 180°C
375°F = 190°C
400°F = 200°C
425°F = 220°C
450°F = 235°C

Find Out More

Books

Adler, David A. *A Picture Book of Frederick Douglass*. New York: Holiday House, 1993.

——— *A Picture Book of Harriet Tubman*. New York: Holiday House, 1992.

Bial, Raymond. *The Underground Railroad*. Boston: Houghton Mifflin Company, 1995.

Hamilton, Virginia. *Many Thousand Gone: African Americans from Slavery to Freedom*. New York: Alfred A. Knopf, 1993.

Kalman, Bobbie. *Life on a Plantation*. New York: Crabtree Publishing Company, 1997.

Kent, Deborah. *In the Southern Colonies*. New York: Benchmark Books, 1999.

McKissack, Patricia C. and Fredrick L. McKissack. *Christmas in the Big House, Christmas in the Quarters*. New York: Scholastic Inc., 1994.

Schroeder, Alan. *Minty: A Story of Young Harriet Tubman*. New York: Dial Books for Young Readers, 1996.

Washington, George. *George-isms: The 110 Rules George Washington Wrote When He Was 14— and Lived by All His Life*. New York: Atheneum Books for Young Readers, 2000.

Web Sites

Colonial Williamsburg

www.colonialwilliamsburg.org/Almanack/places/hb/hbcgrove.cfm

Historic Brattonsville, South Carolina

www.yorkcounty.org/brattonsville/index.html

Monticello, the Home of Thomas Jefferson

www.monticello.org/index.html

George Washington's Mount Vernon Estate and Gardens

www.mountvernon.org/

About the Author

Marian Broida has a special interest in hands-on history for children. Growing up near George Washington's home in Mount Vernon, Virginia, Ms. Broida spent much of her childhood pretending she lived in colonial America. In addition to children's activity books, she writes books for adults on health care topics and occasionally works as a nurse. Ms. Broida lives in Seattle, Washington.

Index

Page numbers for illustrations are in **boldface**.